AMBULANCES ON THE JOB

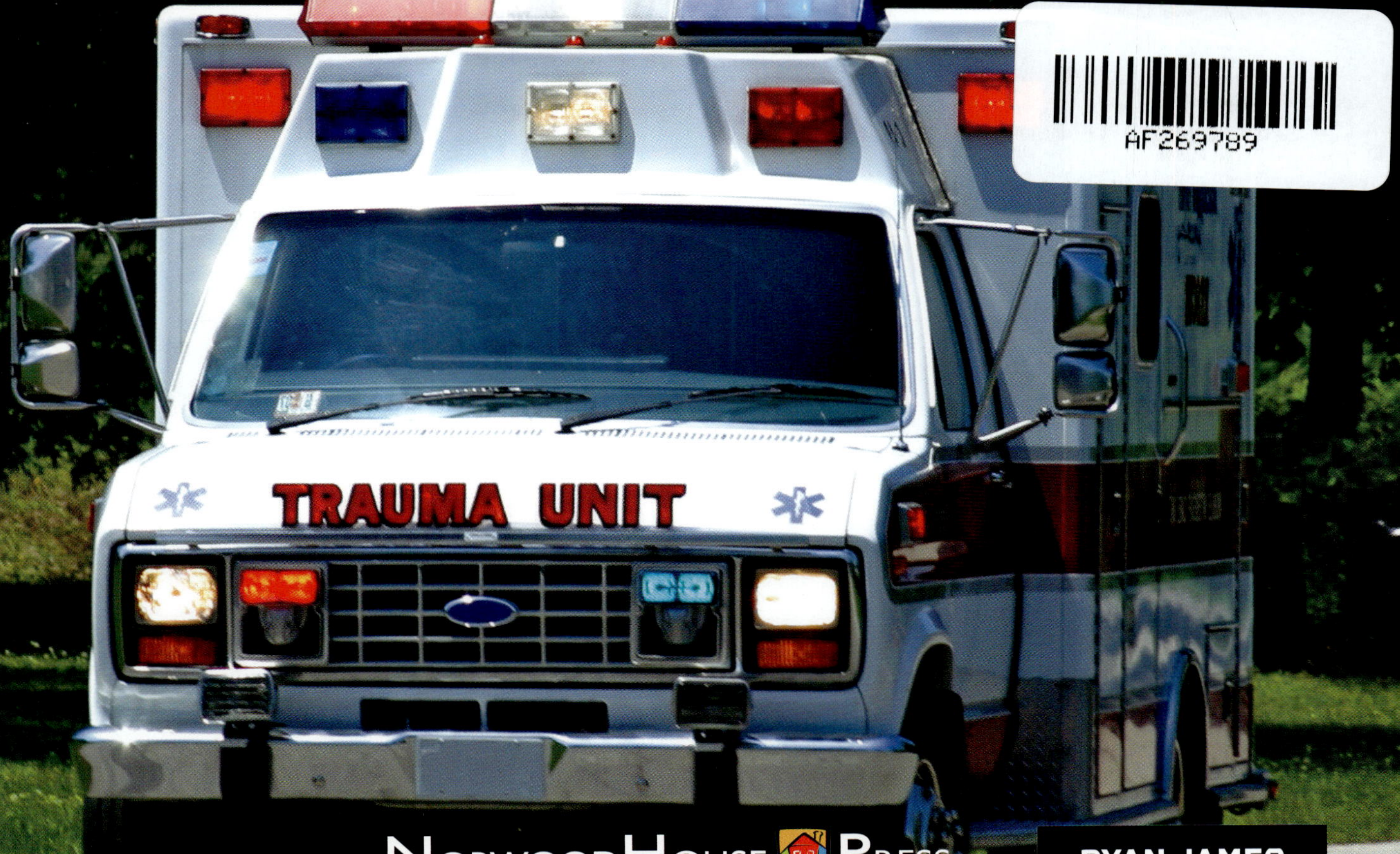

NORWOODHOUSE PRESS

RYAN JAMES

Cataloging-in-Publication Data

Names: James, Ryan.
Title: Ambulances on the job / Ryan James.
Description: Buffalo, NY : Norwood House Press, 2026. | Series: Big machines for big jobs | Includes glossary and index.
Identifiers: ISBN 9781978573758 (pbk.) | ISBN 9781978573765 (library bound) | ISBN 9781978573772 (ebook)
Subjects: LCSH: Ambulances--Juvenile literature. | Ambulance service--Juvenile literature.
Classification: LCC TL235.8 J359 2026 | DDC 629.222'34--dc23

Published in 2026 by
Norwood House Press
2544 Clinton Street
Buffalo, NY 14224

Copyright © 2026 Norwood House Press
Designer: Rhea Magaro
Editor: Kim Thompson

Photo credits: Cover, p. 1 HodagMedia/Shutterstock.com; p. 3 MarekPiotrowski/Shutterstock.com; p. 5 blurAZ/Shutterstock.com; p. 6 Karin Hildebrand Lau/Shutterstock.com; p. 7 My Life Graphic/Shutterstock.com; p. 8 Mirko Chianucci/Shutterstock.com; p. 9 Gorodenkoff/Shutterstock.com; p. 11 Kzenon/Shutterstock.com; p. 12 Dmytro Zinkevych/Shutterstock.com; p. 15 Peakstock/Shutterstock.com; p. 16 F Armstrong Photography/Shutterstock.com; p. 18 OgnjenO/Shutterstock.com; p. 19 Air Images/Shutterstock.com; p. 21 Karolis Kavolelis/Shutterstock.com

Printed in the United States of America

Some of the images in this book illustrate individuals who are models. The depictions do not imply actual situations or events.

CPSIA compliance information: Batch #CSNHP26: For further information contact Norwood House Press at 1-800-237-9932.

Find us on 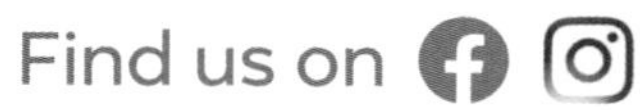

TABLE OF CONTENTS

PARTS OF AN AMBULANCE

An ambulance is a big machine. It has four wheels. It has lights and a **siren**.

1659
F.D. N.Y.
AMBULANCE

The front of an ambulance has a cab. The driver sits there.

The back of an ambulance has tools. There is a **monitor**. There are **oxygen** tanks.

WHAT DOES AN AMBULANCE DO?

Ambulances help people in **medical** emergencies. They work in the city. They work in the country.

Emergency medical technicians (EMTs) ride in ambulances.

An ambulance goes fast. It comes in a hurry. EMTs put the **patient** on a **stretcher**. They lift the stretcher into the ambulance.

EMTs do tests. They look at the monitor.
They find out what the patient needs.

EMTs may give **medicine**. They might put on **bandages**. They may give the patient oxygen to breathe.

Ambulances rush patients to the **hospital**. Doctors work at the hospital. They will help make patients better.

PARAMEDIC
AMBULANCE

AMBULANCE SAFETY

Is an ambulance near you? Listen to an adult. Stay safe so nobody gets hurt.

Do not walk in front of an ambulance. If you are in a car, let the ambulance pass. This lets the ambulance get to the hospital quickly.

Do not bother EMTs. They need to care for patients.

AMBULANCES IN ACTION

Ambulances are **vehicles** on the job.

They help save lives every day!

11963
37
CA EXEMPT
1466637

GLOSSARY

bandages (BAN-di-jis): pieces of cloth or material that protect a part of the body that is hurt

hospital (HAH-spi-tuhl): a place where sick or hurt people get medical care

medical (MED-i-kuhl): having to do with doctors and medicine

medicine (MED-i-sin): a drug or other substance that is used to treat sick people

monitor (MAH-ni-tur): a machine that checks and shows important signs like heart rate, breathing, and blood pressure

oxygen (AHK-si-juhn): part of the air we breathe that helps our bodies work and gives us energy to live

patient (PAY-shuhnt): a person who is getting medical treatment

siren (SYE-ruhn): a device that makes a loud sound to let people know the ambulance is coming quickly to help someone

stretcher (STRECH-ur): a special bed with wheels that is used to carry people who are hurt or sick

vehicles (VEE-i-kuhlz): machines used to move people or things from one place to another

THINKING QUESTIONS

1. What is the job of an ambulance?

2. What tools are found inside an ambulance?

3. Why does an ambulance have both lights and a siren?

4. How can you stay safe around an ambulance?

5. Why are ambulances important?

INDEX

ABOUT THE AUTHOR

Ryan James lives in the mountains of North Carolina where he goes hiking with his dog Bailey. He loves fly fishing, visiting farms in the area, and picking fresh produce. He has always enjoyed writing and wrote his first book as a teenager.